Meet the Orc

Contents   Page

written by Rosalind Hayhoe

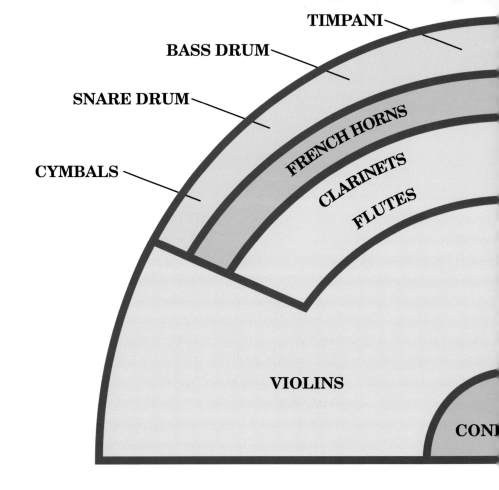

TIMPANI

BASS DRUM

SNARE DRUM

FRENCH HORNS

CYMBALS

CLARINETS

FLUTES

VIOLINS

CON

An orchestra has many interesting and strange-shaped musical instruments, which all make very different sounds. The various instruments in an orchestra are split into four main groups or "sections": the strings section, the woodwind section, the brass section and the percussion section.

The musicians in each section sit together so that they can hear themselves play, with the louder instruments at the back and quieter ones near the front.

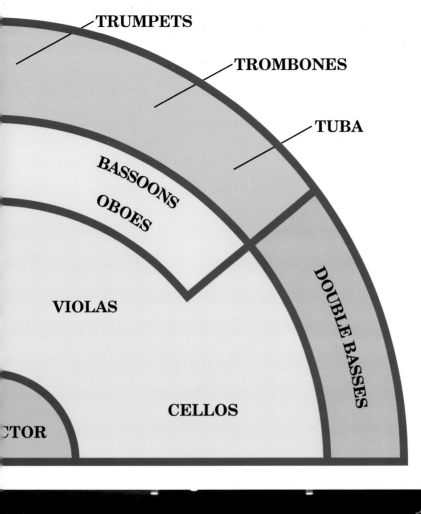

TRUMPETS

TROMBONES

TUBA

BASSOONS

OBOES

DOUBLE BASSES

VIOLAS

CELLOS

:TOR

The Strings section makes up more than half of the orchestra. These instruments are made of wood and their sound is made by a bow pulled backward and forward across the strings. Sometimes the musicians pluck the strings with their fingers. The Violin and the Viola are the smallest instruments in the strings section and have the highest sound. They usually play the main tune for the orchestra. The Cello is much larger and has a beautiful rich tone. The Double Bass is the "grandfather" of the strings section and is so tall that the musician has to stand to play it! It has a wonderful deep rumbling sound and it helps to keep the rhythm of the strings section.

4

Woodwind instruments are long and skinny and are made of wood or metal. Air is blown through a thin piece of wood called a reed or across a mouthpiece to make a noise. Finger holes along the instrument are opened and closed to make the sound higher or lower.

The Flute is a shiny metal tube that makes a beautiful high sound that can be heard above the orchestra. The clarinet makes a smooth gentle sound and is quite easy to learn. The Bassoon is the biggest woodwind instrument and makes very low notes. The Oboe sounds quite funny (rather like a duck) and it takes a lot of puff to play it!

The instruments in the Brass section are made out of long, curly tubes of shiny brass metal, and can make a lot of noise! Sound is made by pressing your lips together and blowing air through them into a cup-shaped mouthpiece. It tickles your lips!
The Trumpet, the French Horn and the Tuba all have buttons called valves, which you press up and down to change notes. The Tuba is the largest brass instrument, and there is only one in an orchestra because it is so loud. The Trombone is played by pulling a slide backward and forward to change notes.

Percussion instruments are very important because they keep the beat for the whole orchestra and are fun to play, as they are either hit or shaken. The Cymbals, Triangle, Tambourines and Drums make sounds that can be either soft or loud, like crashing, tinkling, rattling or rumbling. The Xylophone has different-sized wooden blocks that make different notes when they are hit with small hammers to play a tune.

One of the most important people in an orchestra is the conductor, who stands at the front and leads the musicians. He shows each section when to start playing, and how fast and loud they are supposed to play. Sometimes a conductor waves a pointed stick called a baton to show the musicians how he wants them to play. If he moves his arms in a slow relaxed way, it tells them to play their instruments slowly and softly. If he waves his arms around quickly, then they will play faster. If the music is supposed to be very loud and fast, the conductor waves his arms around wildly!

Apart from these main instruments, occasionally others are used to play certain pieces of music. Quite often a large keyboard called a Grand Piano is added. Other brass instruments like Cornets, Euphoniums or jazzy Saxophones are used, and the beautiful Harp can be included in the strings section, along with acoustic guitars and even electric guitars. Orchestras sometimes perform with a solo singer or a choir.

Music is written in a special language that uses symbols and notations to describe the music, rather than letters and words. It is written on paper called Sheet Music or a Musical Score, and musicians read the music so they know exactly which note to play, and how fast. Each section of the orchestra has its own sheet music so that different instruments play their own tune.

You can learn an instrument at school and join the school band or orchestra. A music teacher will show you how to play your particular instrument and teach you how to read sheet music. It's great fun to learn in a group and make new friends through a shared interest in music. Sometimes the school orchestra will perform a concert for parents and families, or even play the music for the school show.

Orchestras play different types of music:
- Classical music (that may have been written hundreds of years ago by famous composers like Beethoven or Mozart).
- Soundtrack music (written for radio, movies or television).
- Modern music (that might even be played with a Rock and Roll Band).

The music an orchestra plays can sound sad, stormy, peaceful or happy.

Most cities have their own special orchestra, and listening to them perform at a concert is the ideal way to hear and see how all the musicians work together to create such beautiful music. If you are learning an instrument, remember to have a practice every day, and maybe you might play in a famous orchestra, too!